Contents

Introduction

In order to become able mathematicians, children need to develop the ability to discuss mathematical strategies and concepts. Discussing problems helps children to share and focus on ideas; to deal with any difficulties; and encourages a greater interest in their work. Sometimes these discussions are best held between children and teacher, but it is equally important that children have the opportunity to work independently with each other. It is when they talk together, sometimes agreeing and sometimes disagreeing, that children are forced to justify and clarify their reasoning and explanations.

As all teachers know, however, setting up independent group work can be very challenging. Not only must children tackle the maths involved in any given task, but they must also cope with the social demands of a group activity.

Talking Maths is designed to:

- develop children's mathematical thinking and reasoning

- improve children's use of mathematical vocabulary

- build the skills needed to communicate effectively in a group

- ensure all pupils are involved in a group task

- make it easier to set up independent group work in the classroom.

When should I use the activities?

The activities in *Talking Maths* cover each strand of the *NNS Framework for teaching mathematics* and are linked to its objectives. This allows you to select an activity that reinforces and practises skills that have been taught, and that suits your lesson plan. Each activity assumes that the mathematical concepts involved have been previously taught: they are not designed to teach the children new concepts but to provide them with opportunities to further develop their understanding through discussion and to use and apply their skills.

The activities begin by outlining a whole-class introduction, followed by the group task. Suggestions for differentiation should enable the whole class to work on an activity at the same time, making for easier classroom management. Alternatively, the activities can work just as successfully as small group tasks, allowing you to target specific needs in your class. Ideas for a plenary are also provided for the whole class or for individual groups as appropriate. They generally revolve around a discussion of the task: how different groups approached it; what mathematics was learnt; and successful strategies for working together.

How do the activities progress across the series?

The activities within *Talking Maths* are designed to follow a similar format and style from year to year and across Key Stages. This means that similar objectives will be covered and many activities have the same type of structure and aim as a previous activity. There are many reasons for this, all designed to ensure that your school can adopt the activities and develop group work as easily as possible.

- Children need continuous practice at discussing certain key mathematical concepts. Similar activities mean that this can easily be developed and progression tracked.

- If you have a mixed-age class or a particularly wide ability spread then it is easy to find a similar activity above or below the main one for your class to use with some groups of children, still sticking to a whole class lesson.

- Although some tasks from year to year may be recognisably similar there are always several key differences all designed to accommodate the differing abilities and levels of understanding likely to be achieved by a given age range. These may include:

  - an emphasis on different *Framework* objectives

  - different contexts

  - different group sizes or organisation

  - different levels of support in recording work.

How should I group the children?

The first consideration when grouping children is the size for the groups. Many of the tasks suggested in the earlier years of the *Talking Maths* series are suitable for pairs of children, often as an initial stage in larger group work. This allows children to clarify and gain confidence in their thoughts through sharing ideas with one other child, before developing their understanding further in discussion with the group. Later activities in the series tend more to groups of four to six children, with individuals making direct contributions to their group. Although it is tempting to stick with groups of four children, knowing they will feel more confident and are likely to work more effectively, it is important to provide opportunities for larger group work as well. Working in a group of six will give children opportunities to further develop collaborative skills as well as gain extra confidence in discussing mathematical concepts.

You must also decide which children should work together in a group. Some activities provide differentiated resources appropriate for three different ability levels. It is, therefore, sensible to group children according to ability for these tasks. Other activities have differentiation built in, with children responding to tasks according to their understanding and ability to discuss mathematical ideas. For these, it may be worthwhile organising the class into mixed ability groups. This can benefit all pupils in a group: the lower ability children gaining from the ideas suggested by their more able group members, and the higher ability pupils being challenged to make their explanations as clear as possible to ensure all the group are happy with any decisions made.

Finally, it is important to regularly change the way the class is organised so that children feel able to work with anyone and not just a familiar group. As long as the skills required for successful group work are regularly reinforced, pupils should gradually become confident at discussing mathematical ideas regardless of whom they are working with.

How can I introduce and support the group work skills children need?

To allow children to work effectively with each other, it is essential that you learn to take a back seat when discussions are taking place. On saying this, it is clear that children won't automatically work well together and time must be taken to support them in developing the requisite skills. These skills will not appear over night and you must not be disheartened if your children take time learning to work well with each other. It is, however, important to persevere: not only will it benefit the children's mathematical development but also their interaction and success in other areas, both in and out of the classroom.

Introducing and reinforcing group work skills

It is important that the children themselves are aware from the start of the skills they need to develop to be successful in working as a group. If they can take 'ownership' of their developing skills it is much more likely that improvements will happen quickly. Creating an atmosphere in your maths lesson where the importance of working together stands alongside the importance of practising good maths will help children achieve this. The following strategies may be considered in this context:

- **Establishing ground rules**

    Establishing simple ground rules that every member of the group must adhere to is one way of outlining how groups work well together. Once again, this is more effective if the children generate the rules themselves, perhaps through whole-class discussion.

    A class or group poster can be created to display these rules.

- We must share all the information we have.
- We must listen to each other's ideas.
- Everyone in the group must be listened to.
- We must give reasons for why we think we are right.
- We must ask if we don't understand something.
- We must ask each other for reasons for why they think they are right.
- We must agree as a group on what to do.
- We must accept that the group (not one of us) is responsible for what we decide to do and the resulting successes or failures.

As children begin the activities, it can be useful to regularly stop the class, or specific groups, to reinforce the importance of the rules they have agreed upon.

In plenaries of lessons where independent group work has taken place, it is helpful to discuss the social aspects of the task as well as its mathematical outcomes.

- **Introducing 'game type' rules to motivate group work**

    Some children might additionally find it helpful to put 'game type' rules in place to ensure all group members participate. For example, a resource might be provided such as a hat or baton. Whoever is wearing the hat, or holding the baton, is in control of the conversation and must be listened to by the rest of the group. A time limit (using an egg timer) could be put on how long a person can have control of the conversation before it must be passed on to another group member. Children could either request to take control as they have an idea or control could be passed to each child in turn. As children become accustomed to taking turns in discussions the use of the resource can be dropped.

    Additional rules can be put in place when agreement needs to be reached. If a discussion has taken place and there is still disagreement, the children might vote on the line of action they are going to follow as a group. The vote could involve all the children choosing an option on the count of three with an agreement that the winning vote will be adhered to whatever personal opinions are.

- **Modelling appropriate discussion**

    Regardless of established rules, there will still be a temptation for many to plough ahead with personal ideas, disregarding the rest of the group, especially if children are excited by a task.

Modelling discussions can be a useful way of helping children to see how best to approach group work.

Along with a classroom assistant or other adult, try enacting conversations that may take place in a given activity. In particular, highlighting how to provide justifications for your arguments and how to deal with conflict will help children respond appropriately to similar situations. Including examples of situations in your role play where unclear explanations are given, or disagreements are dealt with inappropriately will provide a good point of discussion for the children.

Restricting resources

Deciding what resources will be available and how they will be allowed to be used can further aid the development of group work skills. For example, insisting that children can only read the information on their activity cards, rather than showing it to other members of their group, guarantees that all members contribute to the group discussion. Allowing a group only one set of recording materials can be a similarly successful strategy.

Using contexts

Some children respond well to activities set in a particular context. For example, a task that requires children to deal with a set of clues to find an answer lends itself to the context of detective work. Ask the children to think about how detectives work. Establishing that they investigate and solve crimes by looking for and evaluating clues could help children think about how they are going to approach the mathematical task. This can be particularly useful if you are trying to promote good explanations of ideas and strategies. In most situations, detectives know what crime has been committed and are more interested in how it happened than who did it. Children are often interested in the answer alone and it can be difficult to extract from them the methods and strategies they used to find the answer. If they see themselves as 'detectives', it highlights that the answer is not always enough and how they reached the answer can be of more importance. Building on this, the idea that detectives work in teams and that it is through sharing and presenting ideas to each other that results are obtained, can then help children work together on a problem.

Teacher support

What should your role be when the children are engaged in an activity? You may sometimes choose to join a group for some or all of an activity. This is useful when children are first attempting these activities, as you can encourage the discussions to take place until the format is more familiar. Your involvement should, however, be kept to a minimum as children will tend to value your input above that of their peers. A good way of avoiding this is to assume the role of a group member, becoming a non-expert for the duration of the task. You could, for example, take on the role of a scribe, noting any comments or issues that arise. It is crucial that you do not intervene if the children head down inappropriate paths or if conflict arises, but simply offer opinions based on the information made available to you by your group. Although a difficult role to adopt, if children become accustomed to your presence in this way, it can be a very successful means of observing their interactions and assessing mathematical understanding.

How can I help the children use the right mathematical language?

There are many words that are either specific to maths or take on a different meaning when used in a mathematical context. This can be confusing for children and it is therefore crucial that within any group activity the correct mathematical terminology is promoted within children's discussions. Some of the activities focus in particular on key vocabulary from the *Framework*; others are more geared towards children articulating mathematical ideas as clearly as they can. Assuming that selected activities are relevant to the unit of work being covered in class, then the same vocabulary as has been highlighted for the unit of work will apply to the activity. Useful techniques to support children in learning and using the correct vocabulary include:

- displaying key vocabulary throughout the unit of work and using the display for whole-class activities such as asking children to choose a word and give a sentence incorporating it

- asking children to create their own mathematical dictionary. Any new words introduced at the start of the unit of work must be added to the dictionary along with the child's own explanation of the word. Pupils can use diagrams or example calculations to clarify the meanings of words and ensure they will be remembered. This in itself could form a group activity with pupils sharing ideas of what would be best to record for a given word

- providing a word list to each group at the start of an activity. Children can be encouraged to include words from the list when they are making contributions to the group discussion.

A selection of appropriate key words is listed at the beginning of each activity. They are not intended as definitive lists, as the content of independent discussions cannot be outlined in this way. Rather, they should be viewed as useful starting points or guides through the activities.

How can the children record their work?

Although the main focus of this series is to promote discussion and rich mathematical dialogue, many of the activities can also be used to help children to develop their abilities to record their mathematical reasoning on paper. Possible approaches for incorporating this into activities include:

- asking each group to prepare a brief presentation of how they tackled a problem. This must include written explanations either shown on the board, flipchart or on large sheets of paper that the children can talk through. In the plenary one group can be selected to present their work and others can be asked to comment on it, focusing in particular on how easy they found it to understand the written explanations. A similar task can be set for pairs of children. By working together, children should be able to improve on individual written explanations discussing the best methods of showing their reasoning

- giving an activity to a group and asking individuals to work alone on it initially. They then record their ideas and methods for tackling the problem. Each member of the group must swap their work with another child who must then try to understand and explain it to the rest of the group without help from the original writer.

How can I assess the children's learning?

As already mentioned, taking a back-seat role within a group can prove a very useful vantage point from which to assess the children's understanding. Beyond this, the plenaries should be used to establish how well children have responded to tasks and their level of understanding of mathematical concepts. Whichever activity is being used, you can focus assessment on some or all of the following criteria:

- How well have they understood the task set?

- What evidence is there that they have understood the mathematical concepts highlighted in the *Framework* objectives?

- How well have they explained any methods or strategies they have used?

- How successful have they been at reasoning within a group discussion?

- How well have they worked as part of a group?

- Have they suggested any extensions to the activity, for example posing 'what if …' questions to the group?

With any activity, it may be useful to select one or two groups and carry out a detailed assessment of the pupils within them, choosing different pupils for future tasks. A simple record sheet outlining the points above could be devised and notes made about individuals against each point. This could then be shared with the children to help them in future tasks and can be kept as part of the child's record of mathematical achievement.

How can I follow up these activities in future lessons?

Many of the activities presented in *Talking Maths* can be used for further work with the children. Activities that resulted in children explaining strategies for calculations can be displayed and referred to in later whole-class activities such as mental starters. Others that involved children creating displays of ideas can be added to as their understanding develops, providing a continuing resource up to date with children's learning.

Many *Talking Maths* activities also provide easy to understand games and tasks that, with different numbers, questions or handouts can be reused throughout the year to provide further practise of both the mathematical and group work skills they aim to develop. Further variations on each activity are also outlined on the page.

Equipment needed for the activity

Objectives from the *NNS Framework*

Summary of the activity: key aims and expectations and an outline of any potential problems and prerequisite skills

An introduction to the activity, to be used with the whole class or specific groups, as appropriate

The main group task

Strand from the *NNS Framework for teaching mathematics*

Get in line

Children position and order a set of fractions on a washing line. They need to be familiar with finding simple equivalent fractions. The challenge is to create 'handy hints' to make the task easier for another group. This promotes discussion about how to compare and order fractions and helps children identify useful strategies.

OBJECTIVES

* Order a set of fractions and position them on a number line

RESOURCES

* Washing line and pegs
* Large fraction cards for 0, 1, $\frac{1}{2}$, $\frac{1}{3}$, $\frac{1}{4}$, $\frac{1}{5}$, $\frac{1}{6}$, $\frac{1}{8}$, $\frac{1}{10}$ ... $\frac{1}{12}$ (each punched with a hole centrally at the top and bottom)
* Treasury tags
* A smaller set of fraction cards as above for each group

GROUP SIZE

* 2 or 4 (giving an equal number of cards to each child)

KEY WORDS

number line, strategy, compare, order, equivalent, reduced to, proper/improper fractions, lowest common multiple

Getting started

Use a washing line. Peg the 0 card at one end and the 1 card at the other. Shuffle and give out the large fraction cards. Invite the children with $\frac{1}{12}$, $\frac{3}{12}$ and $\frac{6}{12}$ to come up and hang them on the line in approximately correct positions.

? *Does anyone have a fraction that should hang in the same place as any of these?*

Connect similar fraction cards using treasury tags.

Ask children to hang up the remaining fraction cards starting with $\frac{1}{12}$. Encourage children to explain why they have chosen the position they have, for example, *'It is more than one half but less then three quarters, so I am putting it here'*. As more fractions are placed on the line, discuss how new numbers are compared with the existing ones as well as any changes that need to be made.

? *Is this fraction bigger than this one? How do you know?*

Working together

Each group places 0 and 1 at either end of an otherwise unlabelled number line. They shuffle and share out their fraction cards. Children take it in turns to place a card on the 'line' and justify their chosen position to the rest of the group. As more cards are added, the group must discuss and agree upon any adjustments that need to be made to the position of existing cards.

When all cards have been placed, challenge the group to create a set of hints to help someone else do the task. Encourage children to include guidance on using equivalent fractions for comparison.

Sharing results

Invite a group to show how they have ordered their fractions. Discuss and rationalise any differences amongst groups' decisions.

Share children's strategies for placing the cards and discuss the hints created. You may wish to compile a class list to display for future reference.

? *Is this fraction bigger than this one? How do you know?*

? *How can you find equivalent fractions that make it easy to compare fractions?*

? *Can you think of another fraction that lies between these two?*

Differentiation

Provide appropriate sets of fraction cards for each group.

▼ Use the washing line with some cards already placed.

▲ When the group has completed the task, ask each child to write down a new fraction on a small piece of paper. Children swap papers with each other and position the numbers on the line. Encourage them to be adventurous in their choice of fractional numbers.

? *Can you explain how to find the lowest common multiple you need to compare each pair of fractions?*

VARIATIONS

Order and position improper fractions and mixed numbers, including some equivalents. You will need to discuss and decide on appropriate labels for each end of the number line.

Provide children with decimal cards or measurements to two decimal places, again discussing and agreeing the labels for each end of the line. For example, 4·93, 4·91, 4·99, 5·01, 5·06, 5·04, 4·95, 5·09. Ask them to order the cards on the washing line and then find new decimals to place in the sections between.

Repeat with measurement cards, for example 1·21 m, 1·25 m, 2·25 m, 1·52 m, 2·64 m, 2·70 m, 1·76 m, 2·15 m.

Order cards with fractions as operators, e.g. $\frac{1}{3}$ of 18.

? *Would you rather have $\frac{1}{3}$ of £18 or $\frac{1}{2}$ of £20?*

Relevant vocabulary for the activity

Suggested grouping

Suggested plenary

Suggested variations to suit lower ability and higher ability groups

Alternate ways of addressing the same problem or variations on the problems that can be explored using the same resources

Classroom tips at a glance

- Establish ground rules for groups to follow, for example:
  - sharing information
  - listening to each other's ideas
  - giving reasons for why children think they are right
  - asking if they don't understand something
  - asking each other for reasons for why they think they are right
  - agreeing as a group on what to do
  - accepting that the group (not one child) is responsible for what they decide to do and the resulting successes or failures.
- Model good and bad examples of talking situations and ask the children to discuss them.
- Allow time for paired discussion prior to group or whole class discussions.
- Take a back seat when groups are working or join a group as a non-expert.
- Use 'game type' rules to help children work together, for example passing a baton round with whoever is holding it having a chance to speak and be listened to.
- Allow only one set of recording materials per group to make children work with each other on problems.
- Display key vocabulary and encourage children to refer to it when talking about an activity.
- Provide a word list for groups and ask children to use it during discussions and add to it for future reference.
- Change how children are grouped – get them used to working with anybody!

What am I?

Children use a set of clues to find a mystery number. Each child in the group has a part to play and together they must find the solution. To narrow down the range of possible answers they will need to justify their ideas to each other. Children should be familiar with using tests of divisibility.

Getting started

Write up a selection of numbers less than 10 000. Together practise rounding them to the nearest 10, 100 or 1000.

Remind children how to recognise numbers that are divisible by 2, 4, 5, 10 or, if desired, by 100. Write up the 'rules' for children to refer to later.

You may wish to use the set of optional cards outlined in the *Resources* to model how to find a mystery number. Give children time to consider the clues in pairs. Discuss as a class the best approaches for finding the answer.

? *Were some clues more helpful than others in getting you started?*

? *Have you checked that your mystery number fits each clue?*

Working together

Choose a set of cards for each group, ensuring that each child has an equal number of clues. Children should shuffle them and share them out. Each child may read out their clue(s) more than once but must not show them to the others. Children may ask to hear the clues again. They must use all the clues to find the solution.

When a group claims to have found the mystery number, encourage children to double-check each clue to make sure the number fits them all.

? *How did you decide which clues to use first?*

? *Using each card in turn, can you explain how you are sure your number is the right one?*

? *Did you write anything down to help you?*

Sharing results

Invite a group (or groups) to explain to the rest of the class how they went about solving their puzzle. Discuss and compare different approaches and highlight effective strategies.

Differentiation

▼ Give children a sheet with ten different numbers, including the solution to their puzzle.

? *Can you use the clue cards to find which numbers cannot be the mystery number?*

▲ Ask children to work in pairs to make up their own set of clue cards. Children should swap cards with another pair to solve their puzzle, or their cards could be used as a starter in a subsequent lesson.

? *How can you make sure that there is only one solution to your puzzle?*

? *How can you make sure that every clue is needed to solve the puzzle?*

VARIATIONS

Give each group several sets of clue cards (shuffled, with their set letters blanked out) with matching mystery number cards.

? *Which clues belong to each number?*

Focus on different tests of divisibility and create appropriate sets of clues.

Devise sets of clues that lead to more than one solution.

? *Is there another mystery number that fits all the clues? How do you know?*

Devise sets of clues based on a different topic. For example, to draw a shape that satisfies all the following conditions:

 ● It has 2 pairs of sides of the same length.

 ● It has exactly 2 lines of symmetry.

 ● Its diagonals do not intersect at right angles.

 ● It has equal angles. (Rectangle)

Ask children to create sets of clue cards and use them as a starter in a subsequent lesson.

Save the cat!

OBJECTIVES

- Properties of numbers objectives, depending on the questions posed
- Solve mathematical problems or puzzles

RESOURCES

- PCM 3 for each group

GROUP SIZE

- 3–4

KEY WORDS

property, strategy, between, number range, multiple of, divisible by, square number, greater/less than

In this activity, the children work as a group to identify a number by asking one child questions. With a limited number of questions that can be asked, the discussion will revolve around the information that the children accumulate and the most effective questions to ask.

Getting started

Ask children to visualise a number line stretching from, for example, 5000 to 10 000. Secretly write a number from that range. Children must identify your chosen number by asking questions about its properties, to which you will answer 'yes' or 'no'. (They should not ask direct questions about any of the exact values of digits, for example *Is the tens digit 7?*)

Before they begin questioning you, give children time to discuss in pairs the types of question they might ask. Record each question asked and note which numbers are possible matches.

(?) *What does my answer tell you about my secret number?*

(?) *Which questions do you think are most useful in helping you find the missing number? Why?*

Working together

Draw a large sketch of a cat and remind children that a cat is said to have nine lives. Every time they ask a question the cat loses a life. The aim of the game is to identify a secret number, as in *Getting started*, before the cat has no lives left. After each question children may have one guess at what the number is, without the cat losing a life.

Give each group an appropriate range of numbers to work within and a copy of PCM 3. Invite one child to think of a number within their range and to write it secretly. Other members of the group then pose questions to discover the secret number. The questions should be recorded each time and one of the cat's 'lives' crossed out.

(?) **Which numbers will be left as possibilities after you have asked your question?**

(?) **Can you think of a different question that will leave fewer possibilities?**

Once a group has found the secret number encourage them to discuss which questions were most effective in helping them to 'surround and move in on it' efficiently.

Sharing results

Choose a spokesperson from each group. Hear contributions from each one. Together collate and discuss them.

(?) **Can you describe the times when your group guessed the number successfully? Why did it happen?**

(?) **Which questions were generally most useful? What information did they give you?**

Differentiation

Differentiation is built into this activity, with children asking more effective questions and making most use of the answers to them according to their ability. You may wish to give each group an appropriate range of numbers to work within. Further differentiation could be achieved by:

(▼) Giving each group a prompt sheet of the types of questions that it might be useful to ask.

(▲) Restricting the type and frequency of questions allowed, for example, no 'more than' or 'less than' questions; no repetition of the same type of question…

VARIATIONS

Let children devise their own rules for questioning.

Focus on different number objectives and limit questioning/range of numbers accordingly, e.g. negative numbers, fractions, decimals, percentages.

Base questioning on a different topic, e.g. 2-D shapes.

Use as a whole-class starter in a subsequent lesson.

Top ten facts

Children pool their knowledge and understanding to create a list of 'top ten' facts about a number or mathematical concept. The open-ended nature of the activity stimulates plenty of discussion and the children's recording can be useful for informal assessment, providing a different perspective on their understanding from that of the usual written test.

Getting started

Write up a concept, for example percentages, or a number, such as 23 245. Ask pairs to discuss briefly anything they know about the concept or number. Invite individuals to write one of their ideas under the heading: **23 245**

The number is in the 5x tables.

$23\,245 + 76\,755 = 100\,000$

$23\,000 < 23\,245 < 24\,000$

The sum of the digits is 16 which is a square number.

Encourage children to think about which facts are really useful or particularly interesting in themselves. Display PCM 4 and look for more ideas. Make sure they are ready to tackle the task enthusiastically before they start working together.

Working together

Give each group a number or a mathematical concept to discuss, for example, sequences, fractions, decimals, percentages, doubles and halves, operations, and each pair a copy of PCM 5. They should write the concept/number in the banner at the top of the PCM and work in pairs for about ten minutes to create their 'top ten' list of facts.

Pairs then come together and take turns to present and explain their list to the rest of the group. After discussion of all the contributions the group agrees a list incorporating the best ideas from each pair. Ask children to record the group's top ten facts on large paper for class discussion.

? *Have you included diagrams and examples?*

? *How is this fact or idea useful in everyday life?*

Sharing results

Groups present their charts to the whole class. You may wish to display them and add other ideas over time.

? *Can you explain why you chose to include this in your chart?*

? *Is this idea/fact useful in any other areas of maths/other subjects?*

Differentiation

Differentiation is built into this activity, with children suggesting ideas to the limits of their personal understanding. Further differentiation can be achieved by:

▼ Suggesting children work with a number rather than a concept and giving them a copy of PCM 4 for support.

▲ Giving children a number or concept to tackle that initially may generate fewer ideas, such as zero or negative numbers.

VARIATIONS

Once children have had practice at creating 'top ten facts', they could create their own at the start of each new unit of work to show what they already know. This may then be added to later on, providing a useful basis for assessing the progress made.

This idea may be used for any curriculum area.

Get in line

OBJECTIVES

- Order a set of fractions and position them on a number line

RESOURCES

- Washing line and pegs
- Large fraction cards for 0, 1, $\frac{1}{2}$, $\frac{1}{4}$, $\frac{2}{4}$, $\frac{3}{4}$, $\frac{1}{3}$, $\frac{2}{3}$, $\frac{1}{6}$, $\frac{2}{6}$ ... $\frac{6}{6}$, $\frac{1}{12}$, $\frac{2}{12}$ ... $\frac{12}{12}$ (each punched with a hole centrally at the top and bottom)
- Treasury tags
- A smaller set of fraction cards as above for each group

GROUP SIZE

- 2 or 4 (giving an equal number of cards to each child)

KEY WORDS

number line, strategy, compare, order, equivalent, reduced to, proper/improper fractions, lowest common multiple

Children position and order a set of fractions on a washing line. They need to be familiar with finding simple equivalent fractions. The challenge is to create 'handy hints' to make the task easier for another group. This promotes discussion about how to compare and order fractions and helps children identify useful strategies.

Getting started

Use a washing line. Peg the 0 card at one end and the 1 card at the other. Shuffle and give out the large fraction cards. Invite the children with $\frac{6}{12}$, $\frac{3}{12}$ and $\frac{9}{12}$ to come up and hang them on the line in approximately correct positions.

(?) Does anyone have a fraction that should hang in the same place as any of these?

Connect similar fraction cards using treasury tags.

Ask children to hang up the remaining fraction cards starting with $\frac{1}{12}$. Encourage children to explain why they have chosen the position they have, for example, 'It is more than one half but less then three quarters, so I am putting it here'. As more fractions are placed on the line, discuss how new numbers are compared with the existing ones as well as any changes that need to be made.

(?) Is this fraction bigger than this one? How do you know?

Working together

Each group places 0 and 1 at either end of an otherwise unlabelled number line. They shuffle and share out their fraction cards. Children take it in turns to place a card on the 'line' and justify their chosen position to the rest of the group. As more cards are added, the group must discuss and agree upon any adjustments that need to be made to the position of existing cards.

When all cards have been placed, challenge the group to create a set of hints to help someone else do the task. Encourage children to include guidance on using equivalent fractions for comparison.

Sharing results

Invite a group to show how they have ordered their fractions. Discuss and rationalise any differences amongst groups' decisions.

Share children's strategies for placing the cards and discuss the hints created. You may wish to compile a class list to display for future reference.

> (?) *Is this fraction bigger than this one? How do you know?*

> (?) *How can you find equivalent fractions that make it easy to compare fractions?*

> (?) *Can you think of another fraction that lies between these two?*

Differentiation

Provide appropriate sets of fraction cards for each group.

(▼) Use the washing line with some cards already placed.

(▲) When the group has completed the task, ask each child to write down a new fraction on a small piece of paper. Children swap papers with each other and position the numbers on the line. Encourage them to be adventurous in their choice of fractional numbers.

> (?) *Can you explain how to find the lowest common multiple you need to compare each pair of fractions?*

VARIATIONS

Order and position improper fractions and mixed numbers, including some equivalents. You will need to discuss and decide on appropriate labels for each end of the number line.

Provide children with decimal cards or measurements to two decimal places, again discussing and agreeing the labels for each end of the line. For example, 4·93, 4·91, 4·99, 5·01, 5·06, 5·04, 4·95, 5·09. Ask them to order the cards on the washing line and then find new decimals to place in the sections between.

Repeat with measurement cards, for example 1·21 m, 1·25 m, 2·25 m, 1·52 m, 2·64 m, 2·70 m, 1·76 m, 2·15 m.

Order cards with fractions as operators, e.g. $\frac{1}{3}$ of 18.

> (?) *Would you rather have $\frac{1}{3}$ of £18 or $\frac{1}{4}$ of £20?*

Who's closest?

OBJECTIVES

- Mental calculation strategies: +, −, ×, ÷

RESOURCES

- Whiteboards or scrap paper for each pair
- 0–9 dice per group
- Choose from PCMs 6, 7 or 8 for each group (1 copy for each pair allows for 2 games)
- Timer per group (or children use their own watches)

GROUP SIZE

- 4 or 6 (allowing pairs to play against each other)

KEY WORDS

mental calculation, strategy, operation, add, subtract, multiply, divide

Children perform mental calculations on specified numbers to get as close as they can to a target number in a given time. They play in pairs against other pairs in their group and must each explain and justify strategies to their partner if they are to win. The winning calculations are discussed and checked by the rest of the group.

Getting started

Write: 100, 50, 35, 19, 7, 4. Give children a three-digit target number, for example 464. Ask pairs to discuss how to make 464 using any operation (+, −, ×, ÷) as often as they like, with some or all of the numbers (once only). They should record their attempts on whiteboards or scrap paper. A solution is: $4 \times 100 + 50 + 19 - (35 \div 7)$. Invite children to share results and discuss the calculation strategies they used, first with their group and then with the class.

? *Did anyone find a number closer to 464 than 460...?*

? *What did you think about when you were deciding how to make this number?*

Working together

Each group needs a 0–9 dice and a copy of the same PCM per pair. Pairs must use the numbers on the PCM once only to make a number as close to a target number as they can. They can use any operation as many times as they like. Three children take turns to throw the dice once to generate the three-digit target number, which each pair writes on the PCM. They then start timing two minutes for their calculations. When time is up, pairs compare how close they are to the target number. The closest pair must show their calculations to the rest of the group.

? *Which pair in your group had the number closest to the target? Do you all agree that their number was the closest?*

Sharing results

Invite pairs to show some of the ways they made their target number. Encourage them to use precise mathematical language or diagrams to explain the mental calculation strategies they used.

(?) *What might you try first if the target number was ...?*

(?) *Did you use brackets?*

Differentiation

In trying to get as close as they can to the target number, all children will practise calculation strategies within their own ability. They should work in ability groups to create a satisfying game. PCMs 6, 7 and 8 give progressively harder options for children to try.

Further differentiation can be achieved by:

(▼) Asking children to generate two-digit numbers as target numbers.

(▲) Asking children to generate four-digit numbers as target numbers.

VARIATIONS

Use different sets of numbers, e.g. decimal fractions, negative numbers.

Devise different rules and different sets of starting numbers, e.g. use only addition and multiplication; allow % ...

Calculations for kids

OBJECTIVES

- Calculations objectives depending on strategies chosen.

RESOURCES

- PCM 9 for each group
- Presentation materials, e.g. flip chart and paper, OHP and slides, whiteboards, marker pens
- Practical apparatus, e.g. place value cards, abacus, base 10 materials, interlocking cubes, counters, pegboards and pegs…

GROUP SIZE

- 2–4

KEY WORDS

strategy, method, mental calculation, estimate, check, repeated addition, near double, share equally, solution

Children are regularly asked as individuals to explain the strategies they use for calculating. This can be threatening to some. In this activity groups prepare presentations of calculation strategies for a new television programme about numeracy. Working in a group gives individuals time to formulate and improve upon explanations before presenting them to others.

Getting started

Write up a calculation on the board, for example 5093 – 4989. Ask children to discuss in pairs how they might find the answer. Invite pairs to explain their strategies and record different possibilities.

> **(?)** *Which method have you chosen: mental, mental with jottings or written?*

> **(?)** *Would a diagram, like an empty number line or grid, help you to explain your method?*

> **(?)** *Would your explanation be clearer if you used practical apparatus?*

Ask for children's help in developing ideas for a new television programme about numeracy. Within the programme there will be a regular slot where a group of children explain all the different ways a calculation can be answered.

> **(?)** *How could you make the slot clear, interesting and fun for the viewers?*

Working together

Provide each group with PCM 9. The group must select one or more of the calculations to be 'calculation of the week' for the programme and plan a short and lively presentation of all the different ways they know to solve it. Encourage children to think carefully about the clearest way to describe each strategy they present and to include an explanation of why it works. They should finish the presentation by choosing the 'strategy of the week': the most appropriate one for the numbers in the calculation. Everyone should be involved in the planning and presentation.

> **(?)** *Have you considered both mental and written strategies?*

> **(?)** *Which strategy might be best to use? Why?*

Sharing results

Choose groups to give a presentation.

(?) *Who will now use this group's strategy of the week for this kind of calculation and numbers?*

(?) *How did you feel about working as a group? Did it help you make your explanations clearer?*

VARIATIONS

Challenge groups of children to create television slots about other topics in the same way, e.g. solutions to problems and puzzles about numbers or shapes; making 3-D shapes from nets; creating symmetrical patterns using co-ordinates...

Differentiation

Differentiation will occur naturally in the variety of strategies children use and the quality of their explanations. Further differentiation could be achieved by:

▼ Directing children to specific calculations to give more experience/practice in one area, for example multiplication of a two-digit number by a one-digit number. You may wish to provide them with a proforma to guide recording and presentation.

▲ Directing children to specific calculations to give more experience/practice in one area, for example calculating with decimals. Ask children to include estimating/checking answers in their presentation.

Four in a row

OBJECTIVES

- Estimate by approximating
- Using a calculator

RESOURCES

- Choose from PCM 10, 11 or 12 for each group
- Calculators for each pair
- About 8 counters per pair (different colours for pairs playing against each other)

GROUP SIZE

- 4 (in 2 pairs)

KEY WORDS

estimate, approximation, mental calculation, strategy, product, divisibility, sum, difference, fraction, decimal, percentage

It is often hard to convince children that it is very useful to be able to estimate answers to calculations. Estimation of products is essential for winning this game; children are provided with an ideal opportunity to practise and use this skill for a purpose.

Getting started

Write up a three-digit and a one-digit number, for example 472 and 6. Children work in pairs and approximate to estimate the product. Record all the estimates, asking each pair to justify theirs to the rest of the class. Give one child a calculator and ask them to find the actual answer. Compare the estimates with the answer. Repeat for other examples.

- **?** *Which numbers did you approximate? One of them or both?*
- **?** *Did you round up or down? Why?*
- **?** *Which method(s) of estimation were most effective?*

Working together

Provide each group of two pairs with a copy of PCM 10, 11 or 12 and a calculator. Pairs take it in turns to choose a number from the circle and a number from the triangle, say them aloud and then use a calculator to find their product. If their answer appears on the gameboard they cover it with a counter. The first pair to have four counters in a row (horizontally, vertically or diagonally) wins.

In order to be successful in the game, partners need to estimate products carefully before choosing their numbers from the boxes. Emphasise the need for agreement on which numbers to select each time: they must not take turns to select numbers!

(?) *Which number on the grid would you like to try and cover next? Can you round it to the nearest ten/hundred? Can you see two numbers to multiply to give you this number?*

Sharing results

Invite children to share strategies for estimating products. Talk about strategies for winning.

(?) *Can you think of any other facts about the numbers in each product that will help you to find a close estimate?* (Find the units digit, use tests of divisibility...)

(?) *Do you think there is a strategy for winning this game? Can you explain it?*

Differentiation

(▼) Use PCM 10.

(?) *If you chose these two numbers to multiply, how would you approximate each one to estimate the answer?*

(▲) Use PCM 12.

(?) *Are there closer approximations to each number that will give you a better mental estimate of the product?*

VARIATIONS

Devise similar gameboards and number boxes to find the sum or difference.

Change the sets of numbers available to include, e.g. fractions, decimals, percentages, negative numbers...

Checking answers

OBJECTIVES

- Check with the inverse operation when using a calculator
- Check with an equivalent calculation
- Estimate by approximating
- Use knowledge of sums and differences of odd/even numbers

RESOURCES

- PCM 13 photocopied and cut to provide a set of calculation cards for each group
- Timer per group
- Large paper and marker pen per group
- Calculators (optional)

GROUP SIZE

- 4 (allowing pairs to play against each other)

KEY WORDS

inverse, equivalent, approximate, check, round to the nearest ten/hundred, sum, difference

Children should be familiar with using a variety of ways to check answers to calculations. With pairs playing against each other the more ways of checking that a pair can think of, the more likely they are to win the game. Children clarify their own thoughts by working with a partner and then develop their understanding further in discussion with the group.

Getting started

Write up, for example, $523 + 228 = 751$.

Ask pairs to discuss different ways they could check whether the answer to the addition is correct. Invite children to share their ideas, and list them on the board. If necessary remind children that they could:

- approximate by rounding, that is, the answer must be more than $500 + 200$
- use the inverse operation (using a calculator where necessary), i.e. $751 - 228$ or $751 - 523$
- do an equivalent calculation, for example $500 + 200 + 23 + 28$
- use their knowledge of odd and even numbers, i.e. check that the sum is odd.

Repeat using other calculations.

(?) Does this check tell you if the answer is definitely right?

Working together

Give each group a set of calculation cards to shuffle and place face down in a pile. One child should start the timer as they turn over the top card. In the time allowed, for example two minutes, both pairs must think of as many ways as they can to check the calculation on the card. Suggest that pairs move slightly apart so that they cannot hear each other's discussions. When time is up, pairs take turns to describe a way to check the calculation: the group must agree that each is a sensible strategy and quickly record it. When a pair has no more suggestions, the other pair scores a point. Continue with the remaining cards: pairs take turns to start offering suggestions. The winning pair is the one with the most points when all the cards have been used or lesson time has run out.

VARIATIONS

Devise further sets of calculations cards using, decimals, negative numbers…

Sharing results

Select a card.

? *Can you tell me how I can check this answer?*

? *Does this check tell you if the answer is definitely right?*

If you wish you could ask groups to use their examples to create posters for display showing different ways to check calculations.

Differentiation

Differentiation will occur naturally in the variety of methods of checking children are able to suggest and in the quality of their explanations. Further differentiation could be achieved by:

▼ Directing children to specific calculations to give more experience/practice in one area, for example checking subtraction. You may also wish to provide a prompt sheet of possible ways to check calculations (as listed in *Getting started*). This should be avoided once children are familiar with the activity so that breadth of discussion is not narrowed.

▲ Directing children to specific calculations to give more experience/practice in one area, for example checking divisions.

Operations and words

OBJECTIVES

- Choose and use appropriate number operations to solve problems and appropriate ways of calculating

RESOURCES

- PCM 14 photocopied and cut to provide a set of cards for each group
- Dice labelled +, −, ×, ÷ (leaving 2 blank faces) for each group

GROUP SIZE

- 4 or 6 (allowing for pairs to play against each other)

KEY WORDS

strategy, method, explain, calculate, operation, addition, subtraction, multiplication, division, solution, compare

Children need to build up an 'internal system' for solving problems: understanding the problem; identifying the information needed to solve it; knowing what maths to do and deciding how to do it; estimating/checking the answer; making sure the original question has been answered. They can be helped to do this by identifying and practising one stage at a time. This activity focuses on knowing what maths to do and deciding how to do it; children discuss how to spot clues in the wording of the problem and how to calculate.

Getting started

Pose a one-step problem, for example *I had 26 children in my class last year. This year the number has increased to 31. How many more books do I have to mark for each piece of work?* Allow pairs time to discuss which word/phrase is important in deciding which operation to use to solve this problem.

? *Was anyone tempted to add 26 and 31 because they heard 'increase'?*

? *Can you explain how to decide which operation to use*

? *Which words give you clues about adding/subtracting/multiplying/dividing?*

Working together

Provide a set of problem cards for each group to lay out face up on the table. Pairs of pupils take it in turns to roll the operation dice and select a matching problem. They should justify their choice to the rest of the group. If a blank face is rolled the pair misses a turn. Once each pair has four cards, they discuss their problems and use strategies they are comfortable with to solve them.

(?) *Can you explain why you chose your way of calculating?*

Sharing results

Give each child a problem card, throw an operation dice and ask who has a matching problem. Choose individuals to read out their problems and invite suggestions of ways to calculate the solutions.

(?) *Can you explain why your problem matches this operation?*

(?) *Can anyone suggest a more efficient way of calculating?*

Differentiation

Choosing how to calculate allows more able pupils to discuss the most efficient methods; less able children can use any approach they are comfortable with. Further differentiation can be achieved by:

▼ Asking the group to concentrate on discussing and sorting the problem cards into those to be solved by addition, by subtraction…

▲ Asking the group to go one step further and use their chosen calculations to find the answers. You could introduce scoring. For each problem solved, the score is the numerical value of the solution. The pair with the highest total wins.

(?) *Is there a strategy that will help you win?* (Estimating and comparing answers when choosing which problems to solve.)

VARIATIONS

Note: when you are focusing on one skill used in solving problems, you may not always want children to go on to find the complete solution.

Devise different sets of problems including two-step problems, problems containing unnecessary information… You may wish to focus them on different measures, e.g. time, area/perimeter, and/or vary the sets of numbers used, e.g. fractions, decimals, percentages.

Use the problem cards to practise specific ways of calculating.

Story maker

OBJECTIVES

- Identify and use appropriate operations to solve word problems involving numbers and quantities based on 'real life'

RESOURCES

- PCM 15 photocopied and cut to provide sets of cards for each group

GROUP SIZE

- 4 or 6 (allowing for paired work initially)

KEY WORDS

world problem, number sentence, criteria, explain, inverse operation, addition, subtraction, multiplication, division

Children enjoy creating their own word problems. This is often presented as an add-on activity: some children are excluded and there is rarely an opportunity to discuss how sensible the created problems are, or what skills are used in producing them. Here children work together to create word problems for others to solve. They are encouraged to discuss strategies involved in creating problems that make sense. Children should have had some experience of using brackets.

Getting started

Write up one of the story criteria given on PCM 15. Children work in pairs to write a matching word problem that they may come across in 'real life'. Invite children to read out their problem; discuss as a class whether it makes sense and how it can be solved.

> **?** Can you explain how you created this problem?

> **?** What did you find difficult about creating it?

> **?** Can you identify any good strategies for creating an interesting problem that makes sense?

Working together

Provide each group with a set of cards to place in a pile face down. Turn over the top card. In pairs they create a word problem to match the criteria on the card. Remind children that they must be able to solve their own problem; they should record how they calculated the solution and/or write a number sentence. After a time agreed within the group, pairs take turns to present their problem to the others. The group decides whether each problem meets the criteria and makes sense. They then choose the problem they like best, deciding as a group why they have chosen it. Repeat for other cards.

> **?** Do you need to use brackets to write a clear number sentence?

> **?** What is it that you like about the problem you have chosen?

Sharing results

Select a card and ask groups to read out the problem they wrote for that card. Invite children to explain how they created their problems and discuss the different strategies adopted. Highlight the use of inverse operations.

? *What makes it a 'good' real-life problem?*

? *What is the number sentence for this problem?*

? *What if we put in some (different) units of measure? How can we change the problem and its number sentence so that it makes sense?*

VARIATIONS

Create a display with one of the criteria cards and the different problems created. Use it in an oral and mental starter as a stimulus for making further problems.

Devise further criteria cards to practise working with particular sets of numbers or measures, e.g. fractions, time, mass, area...

Differentiation

The quality of the problems created will vary depending on children's ability and imagination. Further differentiation can be achieved by:

▼ Giving children a limited selection of cards, for example only those involving one operation.

▲ Asking children to work in pairs to create their own criteria cards. Swap with another pair to create a problem to match the card. Children must make sure that it is possible to make a sensible problem based on the criteria they have chosen before swapping cards.

Right or wrong?

Children investigate statements about numbers to find out if are right or wrong. This approach is particularly useful for highlighting ingrained misconceptions; children address these while having to discuss ideas with, and justify them to, each other.

Getting started

Ask children to read the statements on PCM 16. They should think about each one briefly and decide whether it is 'right' or 'wrong'. Use a show of hands to count and record the number of children responding to each option for each statement.

Explain that there is now the chance to think about the statements in more depth and discuss ideas with each other in groups. You may wish to take one of the statements and model how to find examples that support the 'verdict' or not, and how to record these.

Working together

Provide groups with PCM 16. Taking each statement in turn, the children must give their individual thoughts and then agree upon whether it is right or wrong. They must then decide on a group justification for their decision, giving a counter example for 'wrong' and several examples to support an explanation for 'right'. They should make the recording of their examples big enough for everyone to see in *Sharing results*.

> **(?)** *Why do you think this is right/wrong? Can you give me an example that supports your decision?*

Sharing results

Take each statement in turn: quickly compare final decisions with the original decisions. Ask two groups to explain their decision and justify it by showing and explaining their examples. Discuss any disagreement and focus on the clarity of explanations.

Highlight any misconceptions that have been addressed.

> **(?)** *Which statement did you find hardest to decide about? Are you completely happy with your decision now? Why?*

Differentiation

▼ Select just one or two of the statements for the groups to discuss.

▲ Ask children to work in pairs to make up two statements to do with numbers, one right and one wrong. Swap with another pair who must decide which is which.

VARIATIONS

Use the same idea to highlight misconceptions about other mathematical topics, e.g. fractions, probability…

Use statements previously discussed as 'flash' cards for an oral and mental starter: children could respond with 'thumbs up' for right and 'thumbs down' for wrong.

Apply to other curricular areas, e.g. science topics such as forces or properties of materials.

Teamwork

OBJECTIVES

- Use all four operations to solve simple word problems involving numbers and quantities based on 'real life'

RESOURCES

- PCMs 17 and 18 photocopied and cut to provide sets of clue cards
- PCM 19 (proforma to support children's thinking and discussions)

GROUP SIZE

- 2 or 4 (giving an equal number of clue cards to each child)

KEY WORDS

word problems, problem solving, strategy, explain, compare, solution, answer, percentage, fraction

---

Regular discussions of word problems with other children can be really useful in helping children develop independent problem-solving skills. The conversations will help clarify strategies that can be applied to any problem and will build confidence amongst individuals.

Getting started

Remind children of questions to ask when faced with any word problem:

- What is the problem asking?
- What information do I need to solve the problem?
- What maths do I need to use to find the answer?
- Have I answered the original question?

You may wish to model one of the problems with the children. Make large copies of one set of clue cards and display them. Ask pupils to work in pairs to find the answer. Discuss as a class the best approaches for finding the answer.

Working together

Choose a set of cards for each group. Each card states the problem to be solved and one clue to solving it. Groups shuffle the cards and share them out. Each child may read out the clue on their card(s) to the rest of the group as often as they like but may not show the card to other children. The group follows the clues to solve the problem. When they think they have found the answer, encourage children to cross-check each clue in turn to make sure it fits.

(?) *What is the problem asking?*

(?) *Can you solve the problem just using this clue? What other information do you need?*

(?) *Which clue do you need to use first?*

Sharing results

Invite groups to present to the rest of the class the approaches they used to solve their problem. Compare different approaches and highlight successful strategies. Share one of the sets of clues, find the answer together and talk about any difficulties the pair encountered in making sure there was only one solution.

(?) *How did you decide which clues to use first?*

(?) *What maths did you need to use to find the answer?*

(?) *Can you explain how you are sure your answer is the right one?*

Differentiation

The sets of cards are progressively harder; sets A and B are suitable for lower ability pupils and sets E and F for extension. Further differentiation can be achieved by:

(▼) Providing pupils with PCM 19 to support them at each stage of solving the problem.

(▲) Asking pupils to work in pairs to think of a word problem and make up their own set of clue cards. Swap with other pairs in the group to try and solve each other's problems.

(?) *How did you decide on your clues?*

(?) *How did you make sure there was only one possible solution to your problem?*

Rolling dice

OBJECTIVES

- Discuss the chance or likelihood of particular events
- Solve a problem by representing and interpreting data in tables, charts, graphs and diagrams

RESOURCES

- 1–6 dice for each pair
- whiteboards and/or squared paper for recording results
- PCM 20 for each pair

GROUP SIZE

- 4 (allowing for 2 pairs)

KEY WORDS

record, data, represent, tally chart, chart, table, bar chart, bar line chart, likely, unlikely, likelihood, interpret

Children practise representing and interpreting data in tables and charts while focusing on some of the common misconceptions within early understanding of probability. Pairs discuss and justify their ideas to each other and then to their group. Children need to have some experience of the language of probability but, in reaching agreement with others, they will be forced to develop existing views.

Getting started

Show children a 1–6 dice. Ask pairs to discuss which number is most/least likely to appear if you roll it. Invite children to share their ideas with the class and record suggestions, at this stage avoiding any attempts to correct misconceptions.

Least likely might be 2 because I tested and it only came up 1 time.

There's the same chance of getting them all

I reckon 5 because when we rolled the dice randomly 5 didn't come up

? *How can we check which suggestions are true?*

? *How many times do we need to repeat the experiment?*

Working together

Give each pair a 1–6 dice. One should roll it 50 times and the other record the numbers generated. Pairs then collate their data within the group and quickly present it in a table or graph, such as a bar chart or bar line chart.

Give each pair a copy of PCM 20. Ask them to consider each statement in pairs, look at the group data and quickly record whether they think the statement is true or false.

Pairs then join to discuss the statements and reach a group decision on each one. They must be able to justify each decision.

(?) *Does your data support your group decision?*

(?) *If not, can you explain why the data is not supporting your decision?*

Sharing results

Take each statement in turn and invite groups to present their decisions, giving both explanation and justification.

Refer back to children's initial ideas about the truth of the statements and highlight any misconceptions that have been addressed.

(?) *Why is it important to roll the dice lots of times before you come to any conclusions?*

(?) *Were your results what you expected? Why/Why not?*

Differentiation

(▼) Provide children with a blank table to complete as they roll the dice. Give them the first two statements only to discuss.

(▲) Ask children to predict which is the most likely total when two 1–6 dice are rolled. They should experiment to test their prediction and comment on their results.

VARIATIONS

Experiment in the same way with spinners, playing cards, coins, cubes of different colours in a feely bag...

Comparing channels

OBJECTIVES

- Solve a problem by representing and interpreting data in tables, charts, graphs and diagrams
- Use timetables

RESOURCES

- A large copy or OHT of PCM 21
- PCM 21 copied and cut to provide question cards
- Weekly TV schedule per pair

GROUP SIZE

- 2–6

KEY WORDS

collect, data, represent, compare, interpret, table, chart, tally chart, graph, diagram, timetable, duration, mode

An important aspect of data handling is being able to represent and interpret information in tables and charts in order to answer questions. The next step is then to make your own hypothesis. This activity gives children opportunities to develop these skills in the appealing context of watching television. For some questions children need to be familiar with calculating time durations using a timetable.

Getting started

Ask children to suggest ways in which television channels are different. (Focus on terrestrial channels, choosing all five or a smaller selection.)

Display PCM 21: a list of questions you might want to ask to investigate some differences. Choose one of the questions and discuss children's ideas about how to go about answering it.

> **?** *What data shall we collect?*

> **?** *How can we find the answers to the questions easily?* (Present the data in tables, charts, graphs, diagrams.)

Working together

Either assign a question from PCM 21 to each group or allow them to choose one to investigate. Groups collect and represent data for a presentation of their findings. This could be a short verbal report drawing conclusions about what they have found or you may wish to allocate more time to a poster presentation with further charts and graphs.

Discuss steps for working quickly and efficiently:

- Decide what you need to compare, for example all the channels over a whole week, one channel with another, some days of the week for each channel.

  (?) *Have you enough time to do this?*

  (?) *Why have you chosen these channels?*

  (?) *Are you comparing the same days of the week?*

- Decide how you will collect and record sets of data, for instance share out the days or channels among pairs and use the same tally chart or table to record your findings.

- Collect your information individually or in pairs.

- Put all the information your group has collected together and cooperate to find an answer to your question.

- Agree each group member's part in presenting your findings.

Write up a summary as a prompt for children as they work.

VARIATIONS

Use this format to investigate answers to questions on other topics of current enthusiasm, e.g. performance of teams in football leagues.

Sharing results

Groups present their findings to the rest of the class.

(?) *How did you decide what information you needed to collect?*

(?) *How did you collect your data?*

(?) *Why is this a good form of presenting the data?*

(?) *Is there anything else you would like to know/do to be more confident in your answers?*

You may wish to introduce (or remind children of) the idea of using the mode as a way of assigning a typical value to data spread across several days.

Differentiation

(▼) Assign a straightforward problem, for example one requiring data about the number of programmes rather than the time dedicated.

(▲) Ask children to think up their own questions to explore about the TV channels. You may wish them to use a computer program and enter data directly to produce statistics and charts for analysis.

Reading books

OBJECTIVES

- Solve a problem by representing and interpreting data in tables, charts, graphs and diagrams
- Find the mode of a set of data

RESOURCES

- A selection of reading books suitable for two different age ranges, e.g. 5–7 year olds and 7–9 year olds

GROUP SIZE

- 2–4

KEY WORDS

count, record, data, mode, range, maximum, minimum, represent, database, table, compare

Children should be familiar with finding the mode of a set of data. It is important that they are aware of how they can use this skill to test an hypothesis or prediction. Here they look for differences in the text of reading books in order to suggest an hypothesis, which they then test by collecting and analysing data in a simple database.

Getting started

Show children a reading book written for under 7s and one for over 7s. Ask them to take no notice of the story but just look at the text to try to decide which book is designed for which age range. Discuss and record ideas about what was helpful in deciding, for example, the number of words to a page, the length of words, the kind of words, the number of pictures…

Focus on the number of words to a page and the length of words. Invite children in pairs to try and come up with an hypothesis. If necessary give children the start of a sentence to complete, such as *We think that the book for older children will…*

Discuss ideas and agree a suitable hypothesis, for example *We think that the book for older children will have more words on a page and there will be more long words*.

If necessary remind children of how to collect data in a table or database, and how to compare sets of data by looking at the mode.

Working together

To test the hypothesis, give each group a book from each of the two age ranges for comparison. Children need to decide how to cooperate to collect their data efficiently. Depending on the length of the book, they may not wish, or have time, to collect data about every page and so may need to select pages. When they share their results, the group must be prepared to explain which pages they selected, and why. They should agree, and be able to justify, a group response to the hypothesis.

? *What data are you going to collect and how are you going to record it?*

? *What is the most common length (the mode) of the longest word on a page?*

? *What is the minimum and maximum number of words on a page in this book? What is the range?*

Sharing results

Groups present their findings to the rest of the class.

? *How did you decide what information you needed to collect?*

? *How did you collect your data?*

? *What do your statistics tell you about the hypothesis?*

Differentiation

▼ Provide a data collection proforma for the group.

▲ Ask children to create an hypothesis of their own and then test it, for example *There will be fewer pictures in the books aimed at older children.*

? **What does 'fewer pictures' mean? (There could be less space on the page devoted to pictures or the purpose/style of pictures may be different.)**

VARIATIONS

Collect the data from each group to make a whole class database and use it to test the hypothesis in more detail.

Analyse different types of text, e.g. poems and novels, fiction and non-fiction…

What's the story?

OBJECTIVES

- Solve a problem by representing and interpreting data in tables, charts, graphs and diagrams

RESOURCES

- PCMs 22 and 23 for each group

GROUP SIZE

- 4 or 6 (allowing for paired work initially)

KEY WORDS

line graph, distance/time graph, represent, interpret, label, title, axis, axes, scale, units

Children should be familiar with drawing line graphs. It is very important that they also have plenty of opportunities to discuss and interpret them. Here groups discuss distance/time graphs and create stories that they might represent.

Getting started

On the board draw a distance/time graph, for example:

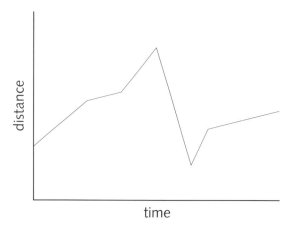

Ask pairs to discuss what the graph might represent. If necessary give ideas to start the children off, for example the story of someone's walk, the distance being how far from home they are.

Invite children to share their ideas with the class. Discuss each one and agree whether the ideas are sensible or not.

(?) What title would you give this graph?

(?) What scale/units would you use on each axis? What if you changed them?

Working together

Provide a copy of PCMs 22 and 23 for each group. They select one graph to focus on. In pairs children create a story to match the information shown by the graph. After an agreed time pairs take turns to present their decisions to the rest of the group. The group decides whether each story matches the graph and is sensible. They then choose the story they like best. Repeat for other graphs.

(?) What did you look for when you were deciding which story you liked best?

Sharing results

When pupils have had a chance to study at least one graph, discuss their ideas within the group or with the whole class.

At the end of the lesson, select a graph and ask groups to read out the story they chose for it.

(?) *Can you explain how you created this story?*

(?) *What do you like/dislike about this story?*

(?) *What did you find difficult about creating the stories?*

Differentiation

▼ Give children PCM 22 only. If necessary provide them with some ideas, for example make up a story about bath time for graph A, a story about going on a day's walk for graph B…

▲ Ask pairs to create a new story and draw a matching distance/time graph. Leaving the graph untitled and unlabelled, swap with another pair who completes it and creates a matching story.

VARIATIONS

Create stories for graphs from science experiments, e.g. temperature/time graphs for melting ice or boiling water, or geography.

Use a distance/time graph to play 'consequences'. Children in the group all start with a copy of the same graph. They write the next stage of the story along the next stage of the graph, fold the paper to hide what they have written (without obscuring the following stage of the graph) and pass their paper onto the next person. Finish by reading out the mixed-up stories.

How long is a piece of string?

OBJECTIVES

- Record estimates and readings from scales to a suitable degree of accuracy

RESOURCES

- Identical set of 10 different lengths of string or ribbon for each group (labelled A–J)
- Measuring tape, metre rule and ruler
- Large copy or OHT of PCM 24 for *Sharing results*
- PCM 24 for groups needing support

GROUP SIZE

- 2–4

KEY WORDS

estimate, measure, measurement, record, compare, length, metre, centimetre, strategy, justify, degree of accuracy

Children should have plenty of practice in estimating lengths. In this activity they must also explain to the rest of the group why they have made the estimates they have, listen to other explanations and come to a common view. Children will need to use comparative vocabulary carefully to give clear justification of their ideas.

Getting started

Show children a length of string. In pairs ask them to discuss how long they think the string is. Ask individuals to come and hold the string and say what they are thinking as they estimate its length. Highlight any good strategies adopted and key vocabulary used correctly.

> **?** *How long do you think 10 cm/1 m is?*
> *Is this piece of string longer or shorter?*

Working together

Give each group a set of strings. Children first estimate the length of each string individually and record their estimates secretly.

When everyone in the group has finished recording, children consider the length of each string as a group. They share and justify their individual estimates of its length, then discuss and agree upon a group estimate. Children must be able to justify their group estimate. Ask them to decide the best way to record their ideas.

> **?** *For this piece of string, will you give your estimate to the nearest 1 cm/10 cm/$\frac{1}{2}$ m/1 m?*

Sharing results

Take each piece of string in turn and ask each group to give their estimate of its length. Agree a class estimate. Record on an OHT or large copy of PCM 24. Invite an individual to choose a tape, rule or ruler, as appropriate, to measure the length of the string. Compare the actual length with the estimates.

(?) *How can you justify your group estimate?*

(?) *What is the appropriate degree of accuracy for measuring the length of this string?*

(?) *Which group's estimate is closest to the actual measurement?*

(?) *Has anyone got any good tips for visualising a 10 cm/50 cm/1 m length?*

VARIATIONS

Use as a whole-class activity for an oral starter to a lesson on measures.

Use the same idea in estimating different measures, e.g. capacity.

Differentiation

(▼) Use PCM 24 to support children's recording.

(▲) Give a set of measurements less than 30 cm. Ask children to draw matching lines using a straight edge with no scale. They can then use a 30 cm ruler to see how close they were.

In between

OBJECTIVES

* Record estimates and readings from scales to a suitable degree of accuracy

RESOURCES

* Sets of objects weighing less than 1kg, e.g. items of food (If you use packaged food items make sure the labelled mass is not visible.)
* Set of weights including 1 kg, 0·5 kg, 100 g, 50 g and 10 g for each group
* Set of scales for each group
* PCM 25 for each group

GROUP SIZE

* 4 (allowing for working in pairs)

KEY WORDS

estimate, heavier, lighter, range, strategy, justify, weigh, scales, mass, record, capacity, length

For older children, there is often little time given to practical measurement and yet they are expected to have a feel for all the properties of a real object. Playing in pairs against other pairs, here children practise estimating the mass of different objects. They must justify each estimate clearly to each other with appropriate and precise mathematical language.

Getting started

Show the children a set of weights and an object. Invite individuals to hold the weights and the item and to estimate a range for the mass of the object, for example between 50 g and 80 g. Ask children to say what they are thinking as they estimate the mass. Highlight any good strategies adopted and key vocabulary used correctly.

> **(?)** *Which feels heavier, the object or the 1 kg weight?*

> **(?)** *Does the mass of the object lie between the 1 kg and 0·5 kg weights?*

Working together

Give each group a collection of objects, a set of weights and scales. Pairs take an object and estimate a range for its mass. When each pair has made an estimate, the group uses the scales to weigh the object and each pair checks whether this mass is within their estimated range. If so, the pair scores one point. The pair with the narrowest correct range scores an extra two points.

Repeat for other objects. As groups finish with a set of objects, swap them for another group's set. Aim for most of the groups to estimate the mass of most of the objects. You may wish groups to use PCM 25 for recording.

Sharing results

Use some or all of the items and invite groups to say which pair had the narrowest correct range. Encourage children to share the strategies they used to make their estimates highlighting good ideas and use of language.

(?) *Can you pick one weight that you are confident is heavier/lighter than the item?*

(?) *By putting weights together can you make a better estimate?*

Differentiation

Differentiation occurs naturally as some children are able to narrow down their estimated range more successfully than others. A point is scored for giving a correct range, however wide, and so children who are only confident with a wide range will still achieve success. The extra points available for a narrower range will motivate the more able to be as accurate as they can. Further differentiation can be provided by:

▼ Asking children to find the weight they think is nearest to the mass of the object and record whether the object is heavier or lighter than the weight before they make an estimate of range.

▲ Provide only a 1 kg weight to aid children in making their estimates. Once pairs have agreed upon an estimated range for each item, provide other weights so that they can reassess their estimates.

VARIATIONS

Estimate capacities instead of masses. Provide each group sight of differently shaped measuring beakers/cylinders filled to 1 litre, 500 ml, 100 ml, 10 ml.

Provide a circus of activities estimating a range of possible measurements in different contexts, e.g. numbers of beads in different jars, lengths of wool/ribbon, capacity of different beakers, weight of cereal bars, solutions to calculations…

Make this shape

OBJECTIVES

- Visualise 3-D shapes from 2-D drawings

RESOURCES

- Choose from PCM 26, 27 or 28 photocopied to provide a set of visualisation cards for each group
- 10 interlocking cubes for each child

GROUP SIZE

- 2–4

KEY WORDS

2-D/two-dimensional, 3-D/three-dimensional, shape, cube, cuboid, cylinder, build, construct, next to, above, below, behind

One child looks at a 2-D representation of a 3-D shape and gives instructions for making it to the rest of their group. This can be a very useful means of developing the individual's confidence in using mathematical language. Other children practise listening carefully and responding accurately.

Getting started

Provide pairs of children with a set of interlocking cubes. Secretly select one of the shapes on PCM 26. Give children instructions for putting their cubes together to make the shape. Ask pairs to hold up their shape after each instruction and identify any misinterpretation of language. Compare the completed shapes with the picture on the card.

(?) *Which words help you decide where to put the next cube?*

(?) *What makes a good instruction?*

Working together

Give each group a set of cards to shuffle and place face down in a pile. Each child needs 10 cubes and a screen to work behind, for instance an open file. Children take turns to pick up the top card and secretly look at the picture of the 3-D shape. They then give instructions to the other children for making the shape. The group discusses and compares the finished shapes with the picture on the card.

Sharing results

Together summarise the features of a good instruction.

(?) *What did you find most difficult when instructing the rest of your group?*

(?) *Which shape was the most/least successful?*

(?) *Which instructions were the easiest/hardest to follow?*

Differentiation

(▼) Give children a set of cards made from PCM 26

(▲) Give children a set of cards made from PCM 28

VARIATIONS

Use the activity as a whole-class oral starter.

Devise cards with pictures of everyday objects that are made of recognisable 3-D shapes, e.g. a table:

(?) *Imagine a cuboid about $1\frac{1}{2}$ m long, 1 m wide and 2 cm thick placed horizontally on top of 4 slim cylinders about 1 m high.*

Children draw what they see in their heads and try to name the object as it is described. Approximate measurements should be given.

Children use rhombi made of congruent equilateral triangles in 3 colours to create their own 2-D representations of shapes made with interlocking cubes for other children to build in 3-D.

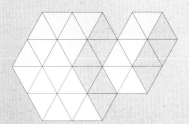

Testing statements

OBJECTIVES

- Investigate a general statement about familiar shapes
- Recognise properties of rectangles

RESOURCES

- PCM 29 for each child
- Large paper and marker pens for each group

GROUP SIZE

- 2–4

KEY WORDS

investigate, record, compare, explain, justify, property, regular, irregular, perimeter, area, symmetrical, angle, right-angled

Children investigate statements about shapes. They think about whether each is always true, sometimes true or false. This approach is particularly useful for highlighting ingrained misconceptions: children address these while having to discuss ideas with, and justify them to, each other.

Getting started

Ask children to read the statements on PCM 29. They should think about each one briefly and write one of: always true; sometimes true; false. Use a show of hands to count and record the number of children responding to each option for each statement.

Explain that there is now the chance to think about the statements in more depth and discuss ideas with each other in groups. You may wish to take one of the statements and model how to find examples that support the 'verdict' or not, and how to record these.

Working together

Children work in groups and take each statement in turn. They share their individual thoughts and then come to an agreement on whether the statement is always true, sometimes true or false (never true). They must decide on a group justification for their decision, giving one counter example for 'false', one of each for 'sometimes true' and several examples to support an explanation for 'true'. They should make the recording of their examples big enough for everyone to see in *Sharing results*.

(?) *Why do you think this is true/ sometimes true/false? Can you give me an example that supports your decision?*

Sharing results

Take each statement in turn. Ask groups to explain their decision and justify it by showing and explaining their examples. Discuss any disagreement and focus on the clarity of explanations.

Highlight any misconceptions that have been addressed. Compare final decisions with the original decisions.

(?) *Which statement did you find hardest to decide about?*

(?) *Are you completely happy with your decision now? Why?*

Differentiation

(▼) Select just one or two of the statements for the groups to discuss.

(▲) In pairs, ask children to make up two statements to do with shapes, one true and one false. Swap with another pair who must decide which is which.

VARIATIONS

Devise different sets of statements about the properties of 2-D or 3-D shapes.

Use statements previously discussed as 'flash' cards for an oral and mental starter: children could respond with 'thumbs up' for true, 'thumbs down' for false and 'thumbs together' for sometimes true.

Use the same idea to highlight misconceptions about other mathematical topics, e.g. fractions, probability.

Apply to other curricular areas, e.g. science topics such as forces or properties of materials.

What am I?

A I am 3780 rounded to the nearest 10.

A I am an odd number.

A The difference between my thousands digit and my units digit is 2.

A My tens digit is larger than my hundreds digit.

B I am 6700 rounded to the nearest 100.

B I am divisible by 4.

B My hundreds digit is the same as my thousands digit.

B The sum of my digits is 24.

C I am divisible by 4.

C I am 7500 rounded to the nearest 100.

C The difference between my hundreds digit and my thousands digit is 3.

C The sum of my digits is 21.

D I am divisible by 5.

D I am 2500, rounded to the nearest hundred.

D The sum of my digits is 17.

D The difference between my tens digit and my hundreds digit is 2.

E All my digits are even.

E I am 5000, rounded to the nearest thousand.

E My tens digit is four more than my units digit.

E The sum of my digits is 20.

F My units digit is 4.

F I am 10 000, rounded to the nearest 1000.

F My hundreds digit is 6.

F The sum of my digits is 24.

Save the cat!

Name: _____

	Question	Answer (Yes/No)	Guess
1	_____	_____	_____
2	_____	_____	_____
3	_____	_____	_____
4	_____	_____	_____
5	_____	_____	_____
6	_____	_____	_____
7	_____	_____	_____
8	_____	_____	_____
9	_____	_____	_____

Top ten facts

About a number, for example 23 245

Try to come up with useful or interesting facts. Think about:

- what the digits in the number stand for

- rounding or ordering the number

- properties of the number, e.g. whether it is odd or even, which numbers it is divisible by…

- things you could do with the number, e.g. doubling

- calculations involving the number

- 'story' problems involving the number.

About a concept, for example percentages

Try to show what you understand about the mathematical idea or concept. Think about:

- diagrams that help you explain what you mean

- examples of numbers or calculations that help you explain your ideas

- how the concept links to others, e.g. which percentages are equivalent to which fractions or decimals

- how the concept can be useful in real life.

When you are choosing your top ten facts, decide which ones you like best and why.

Top ten facts

Name: _____

10 _____

9 _____

8 _____

7 _____

6 _____

5 _____

4 _____

3 _____

2 _____

1 Our favourite fact is…

Who's closest?

Name: _____

9	20	100
8	3	15

Target

Calculations

9	20	100
8	3	15

Target

Calculations

Who's closest?

Name: _____

100	19	50
7	4	35

Target

Calculations

100	19	50
7	4	35

Target

Calculations

Who's closest?

Name: _____

99	25	8
3	51	32

Target

Calculations

99	25	8
3	51	32

Target

Calculations

Calculations for kids

Name: _____

548 + 675
645 – 286
4128 – 2485
7648 + 1495
6·4 + 3·8

72 × 6
172 ÷ 4
35 × 14
248 × 9
256 ÷ 8

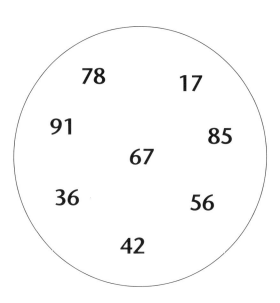

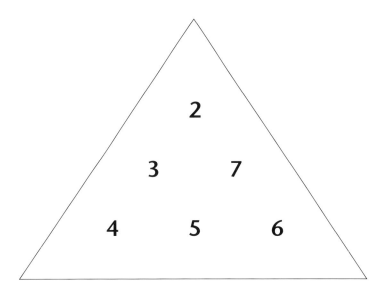

Gameboard

637	144	112	273	468	85	268	84
170	119	234	280	126	455	34	402
546	364	168	312	510	469	156	72
390	392	252	595	68	335	108	255
102	425	224	134	216	294	336	210

Four in a row

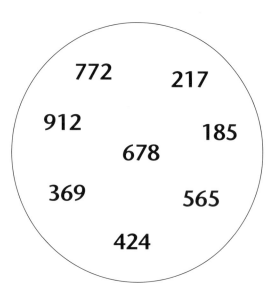

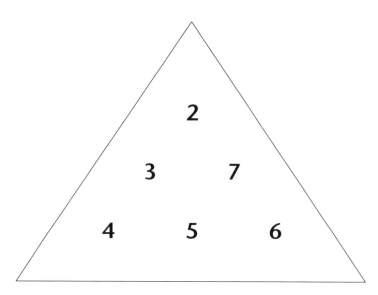

Gameboard

2316	555	1696	3955	4746	1519	370	4632
2712	1107	1130	5404	868	2214	1824	1295
5472	740	1356	3088	2120	2260	1302	1845
434	1695	2968	1085	738	925	1272	3860
2736	1476	6384	3390	848	4560	4068	2034

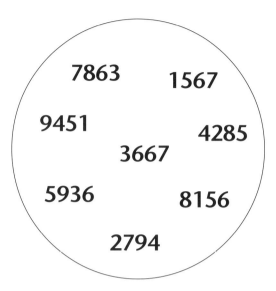

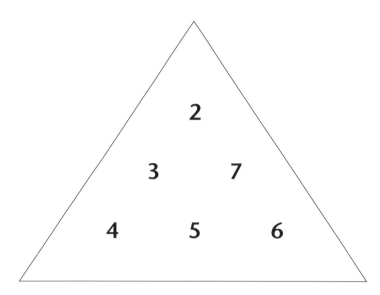

Gameboard

15 726	4701	66 157	22 002	21 425	35 616	19 558	16 312
47 255	25 710	11 872	31 452	40 780	11 001	18 902	3134
18 335	29 680	8382	32 624	9402	39 315	8570	5588
6268	25 669	41 552	11 176	24 468	17 140	37 804	55 041
57 092	29 995	56 706	10 969	23 589	14 668	17 808	16 764

$$3765 - 986 = 2779$$

$$1650 \div 50 = 33$$

$$2600 + 1345 = 3945$$

$$83 \times 9 = 747$$

$$534 + 278 = 812$$

$$24 \times 19 = 456$$

$$607 - 196 = 411$$

$$3428 + 4136 = 7564$$

$$2743 - 437 = 2306$$

$$73 \times 11 = 803$$

You may wish to enlarge to A3 for copying and cutting.

Boxes hold 12 eggs. How many boxes are needed for 216 eggs?	384 people have booked a seat on the non-stop train from Nottingham to York. There are 54 seats in each carriage and no standing is allowed. How many carriages are needed?	Steve has played 2 rounds of his new computer game. He scored 468 and 276. What is his total score so far?	There were 400 visitors to the museum in June, 700 in July and 500 in August. How many visitors were there in the June to August quarter of the year?
There are 21 rows of chairs in the hall. Each row holds 13 chairs. How many children can sit on chairs in the hall?	In one year at the nature reserve there were 587 sightings of sparrows and 475 sightings of robins. How many sightings of the two birds were there altogether?	In a sponsored walk, Arash, Harry and Ryan each walked 4·9 km. How many kilometres did they walk in total?	The school has 90 m of cloth to make covers for tables at the school fair. It takes 6 m of cloth to cover each table. How many tables can be covered?
There were 6483 supporters at the football match. 2860 of them were male. How many supporters were female?	In a talent contest, Nadia came first with 754 votes and Rukhsana came second with 286 votes. By how many votes did Nadia win?	Mrs Davids has a box of chocolates to share amongst her class. There are 69 chocolates and 23 children in the class. How many chocolates can each child have?	How many days are there in 46 weeks?
The total number of visitors to the water sports centre last year was 7864. This year there were 678 more visitors than last year. How many visitors were there this year?	The local hospital sold 4362 raffle tickets to patients and visitors. The radio station sold another 1485 tickets. How many tickets were sold altogether?	There are 40 apple trees in an orchard. The total number of apples produced last year was about 3600. About how many apples did each tree produce?	A Christmas cracker factory makes 456 boxes of crackers each month. How many boxes of crackers are produced in 8 months?
7 children each deliver 86 leaflets advertising a new car wash. What is the total number of leaflets they delivered?	Margaret was born in January 1929. She gave birth to her son Jake in February 1967. How old was Margaret when Jake was born?	Emma had a new video game. She scored 562 points on her first go and 863 points on her second go. By how many points did her score improve?	In a zoo there is an elephant who weighs 5236 kg and a lion who weighs 213 kg. How much heavier than the lion is the elephant?

Answer: 273

Solve using subtraction only

Answer: 3600

Solve using multiplication only

Answer: 970

Solve using multiplication and addition only

Answer: 16

Solve using division only

Answer: 40

Include percentages

Answer: 122

Solve using at least two mathematical operations

Answer: 32

Solve using multiplication and division only

Include weight

Solve using two mathematical operations only

Include decimals

Solve using at least two mathematical operations

Answer: 8

Include fractions

Solve using at least two mathematical operations

Right or wrong?

A multiple of 8 is both a multiple of 2 and a multiple of 4.

The total of three consecutive numbers is always even.

If you change the order of dividing two different numbers the answer stays the same.

A number is a multiple of 9 if its digits add up to 9.

The product of two consecutive numbers is always even.

The difference between two odd numbers is always odd.

A *In a talent contest Sean, Nadeem, Tom and Ali got the most votes. Who won and by how much?*
Sean got 487 votes.

A *In a talent contest Sean, Nadeem, Tom and Ali got the most votes. Who won and by how much?*
Tom got 86 more votes than Sean.

A *In a talent contest Sean, Nadeem, Tom and Ali got the most votes. Who won and by how much?*
Nadeem got 342 votes.

A *In a talent contest Sean, Nadeem, Tom and Ali got the most votes. Who won and by how much?*
Ali got 146 more votes than Nadeem.

B *How many free minutes has Sarah got left on her mobile phone?*
When Sarah bought her phone she was given 240 free minutes.

B *How many free minutes has Sarah got left on her mobile phone?*
So far, Sarah has used up 86 minutes on personal calls.

B *How many free minutes has Sarah got left on her mobile phone?*
Sarah paid for an extra 60 minutes of talk time.

B *How many free minutes has Sarah got left on her mobile phone?*
Sarah's business calls have used up 47 minutes.

C *Claire, Mark, Kate and Dean wash cars for a day for charity. How many buckets of water do they use?*
It takes 7 buckets of water to wash a car.

C *Claire, Mark, Kate and Dean wash cars for a day for charity. How many buckets of water do they use?*
Mark washed 16 cars during the day.

C *Claire, Mark, Kate and Dean wash cars for a day for charity. How many buckets of water do they use?*
Claire washed 21 cars during the day.

C *Claire, Mark, Kate and Dean wash cars for a day for charity. How many buckets of water do they use?*
Kate and Dean washed cars together. They washed 5 times as many cars as Mark.

D Sanjeev and Jack were playing a computer game. Who won and by how many points?
Sanjeev scored 2304 points on level 1.

D Sanjeev and Jack were playing a computer game. Who won and by how many points?
Sanjeev scored 3562 points on level 2.

D Sanjeev and Jack were playing a computer game. Who won and by how many points?
Jack had a total score of 4586 by the end of level 2.

D Sanjeev and Jack were playing a computer game. Who won and by how many points?
Sanjeev and Jack scored the same points on the third, and final, level.

E Sunita took part in a sponsored walk. How much money did she raise for charity?
Sunita walked 8 miles.

E Sunita took part in a sponsored walk. How much money did she raise for charity?
Sunita had 65 sponsors.

E Sunita took part in a sponsored walk. How much money did she raise for charity?
People sponsored Sunita 25p per mile.

E Sunita took part in a sponsored walk. How much money did she raise for charity?
If Sunita raised over £100, her school promised to add 25% of the amount she raised to her total.

F How many bottles of squash need to be bought for the school Christmas party?
One bottle of squash is enough for 32 drinks.

F How many bottles of squash need to be bought for the school Christmas party?
Each child is allowed 3 drinks during the party.

F How many bottles of squash need to be bought for the school Christmas party?
256 children will be at the party.

F How many bottles of squash need to be bought for the school Christmas party?
There will be 16 adults supervising; they are each allowed 2 drinks.

Teamwork

Name: _____

The problem:

Key words and numbers in the problem:

Calculation(s) needed:	Jottings/Written method:

Answer:

Units required for answer:

Rolling a 1-6 dice

Name: _____

I am less likely to roll a 6 than any other number.	
I am more likely to roll 1, 2 or 3 than 4, 5 or 6.	
If I rolled the dice another 60 times I would get each number about another 10 times.	
If I rolled three 6s in a row, the next roll is less likely to be 6 than any other number.	
I am more likely to roll an even number than an odd number.	

Which channel spends most time on sport?

Which channel shows most children's programmes?

How much more time does BBC1 dedicate to children's television than BBC2?

Which channel shows the most news programmes in a day?

How many hours a week does each channel spend on news programmes?

Do all channels show the same types of programmes between 5pm and 7pm on weekdays?

Does the BBC dedicate the same amount of time to children's programmes on weekdays as it does at the weekend?

Which channel shows most quiz programmes?

Are more films shown on some channels than others?

Do some channels spend more time on soap operas than others?

Name: _____

A

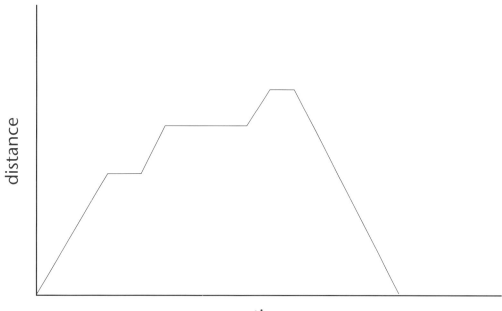

distance

time

B

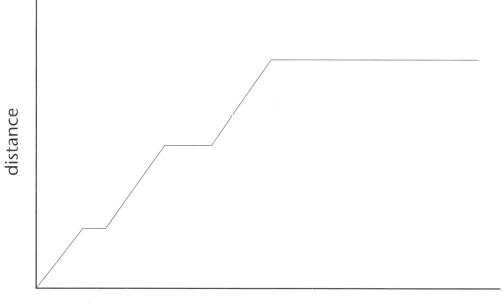

distance

time

Name: _____

C

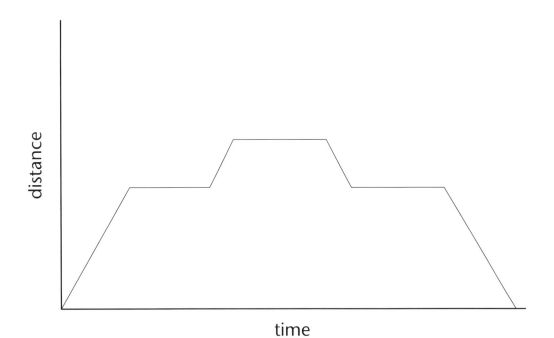

D

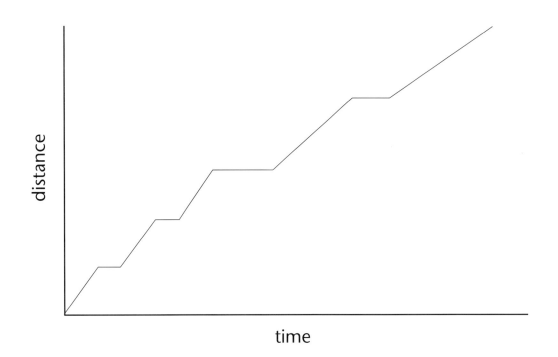

How long is a piece of string?

Name: _____

About how long?

String	Estimate 1	Estimate 2	Estimate 3	Estimate 4	Agreed estimate	Actual length
A						
B						
C						
D						
E						
F						
G						
H						
I						
J						

In between

Scores

Names	Names										

About how heavy?

Object	Names		Actual weight								
	Between... and...	Between... and...									

Make this shape

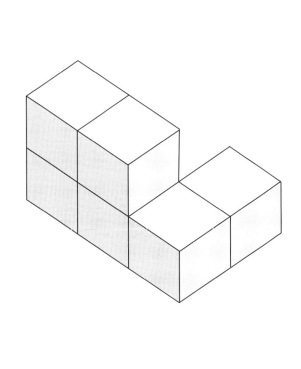

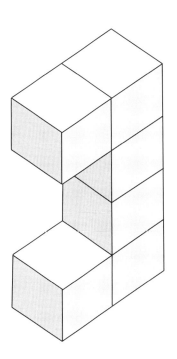

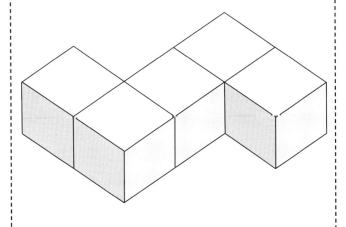

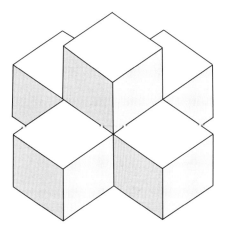

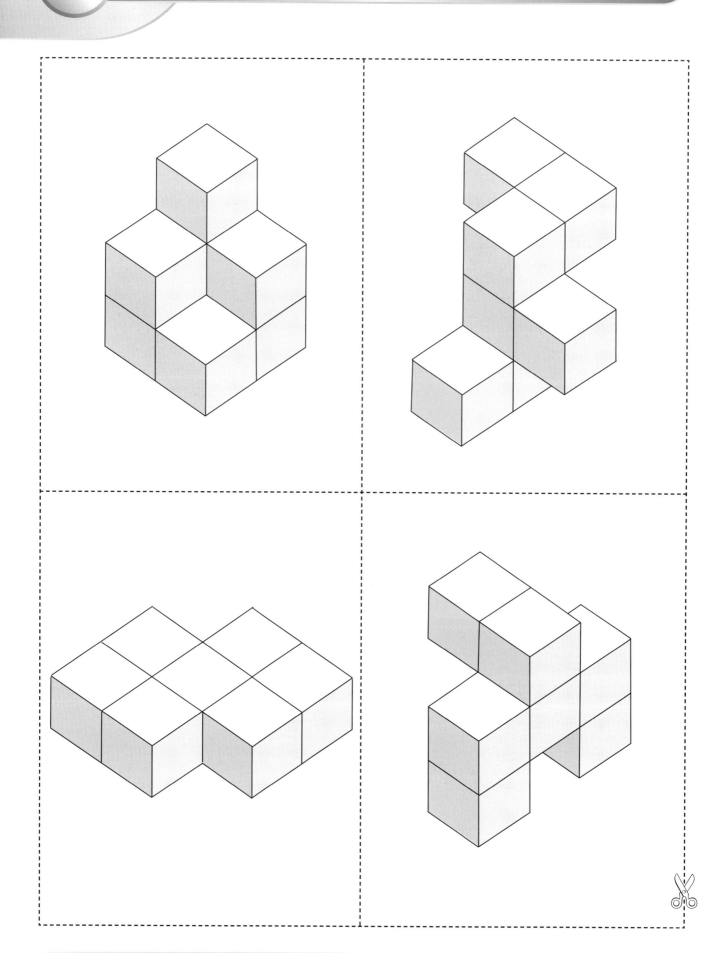

Make this shape

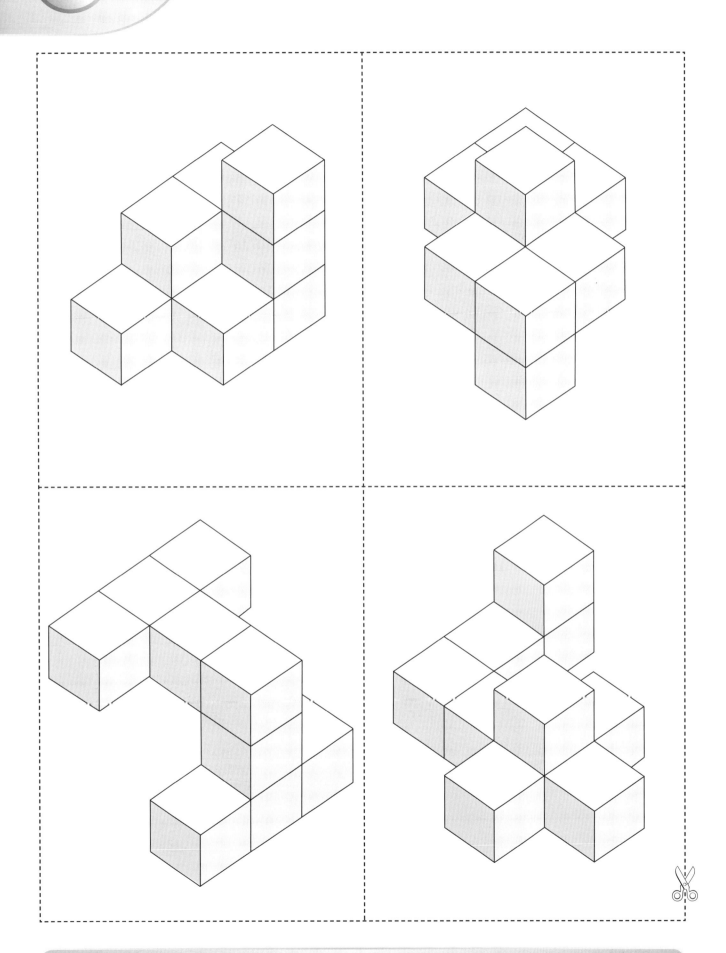

The perimeter of a regular polygon is length of sides multiplied by the number of sides.

If the sides are whole cm in length, it is possible to make 6 different rectangles with an area of $24\,\text{cm}^2$.

The larger the perimeter of a rectangle, the larger the area.

All equilateral triangles tessellate.

The angles on a straight line add up to $180°$.

The diagonals of any rectangle intersect at right angles.

The number of lines of symmetry in a polygon is equal to the number of sides.

A regular hexagon has six diagonals.

Unit plans

Activity	NNS Framework	Autumn 1	Autumn 2	Autumn 3	Autumn 4	Autumn 5	Autumn 6a	Autumn 6b	Autumn 8	Autumn 9	Autumn 10	Autumn 11	Autumn 12	Spring 1	Spring 2	Spring 3	Spring 4	Spring 5a	Spring 5b	Spring 7	Spring 8	Spring 9	Spring 10	Spring 11	Summer 1	Summer 2	Summer 3	Summer 4	Summer 5	Summer 6a	Summer 6b	Summer 8	Summer 9	Summer 10	Summer 11	Summer 12
What am I?	pp 3, 11, 13, 19, 77, 79	●																													●					●
Save the cat!	pp 17, 19, 21, 79								●				●																		●					●
Top ten facts	pp 2–33	●			●								●	●															●							●
Get in line	p 23				●																															
Who's closest?	pp 40–47, 60–65									●		●			●							●					●								●	
Calculations for kids	pp 38–73			●			●					●			●	●						●	●		●		●								●	
Four in a row	pp 11, 13, 71, 73	●						●		●					●										●											
Checking answers	pp 11, 13, 19, 73			●								●													●											●
Operations and words	p 75			●																		●					●									
Story maker	pp 82–89			●							●												●	●		●								●		
Right or wrong?	p 81											●						●						●												●
Teamwork	pp 82–89			●					●		●	●			●	●							●			●								●		
Rolling dice	pp 113, 115, 117						●	●						●							●									●						
Comparing channels	pp 99, 101, 115, 117						●	●						●							●									●				●		
Reading books	pp 115, 117						●	●						●							●									●						
What's the story?	pp 115, 117						●							●							●									●						
How long is a piece of string?	pp 93, 95																			●													●			
In between	pp 93–95											●						●		●												●	●			
Make this shape	p 105								●									●														●				
Testing statements	pp 81, 103								●				●					●														●	●			

Talking Maths and 5-14

Talking Maths Year 5 is suitable for use mainly at levels C and D. All of its activities draw on and develop skills in problem-solving and enquiry at these levels.

Talking Maths activity	Mathematics 5–14 reference	
	Strand	Level
What am I?	Range and type of numbers	C
	Round numbers	D
	Multiply and divide	C
Save the cat!	Range and type of numbers	C
Top ten facts	Range and type of numbers	D
Get in line	Range and type of numbers	D
Who's closest?	Add and subtract	C
	Multiply and divide	C
Calculations for kids	Add and subtract	C/D
	Multiply and divide	C/D
Four in a row	Multiply and divide	C
	Round numbers	D
Checking answers	Add and subtract	D
	Multiply and divide	C/D
	Round numbers	D
Operations and words	Add and subtract	D
	Multiply and divide	D
Story maker	Add and subtract	D
	Multiply and divide	D
	Fractions, percentages and ratio	D
Right or wrong?	Range and type of numbers	C/D
	Multiply and divide	C
Teamwork	Add and subtract	C
	Multiply and divide	C
Rolling dice	Information handling: collect	C
	Information handling: organise	C
	Information handling: display	C
	Information handling: interpret	C/D
Comparing channels	Information handling: collect	D
	Information handling: organise	D
	Information handling: display	C
	Information handling: interpret	D
	Time	C/D
Reading books	Information handling: collect	D
	Information handling: organise	D
	Information handling: interpret	D/E
What's the story?	Information handling: display	D
	Information handling: interpret	D
How long is a piece of string?	Measure and estimate	C
In between	Measure and estimate	D
Make this shape	Range of shapes	C/D
Testing statements	Range of shapes	C/D
	Symmetry	D
	Angle	C